THIS DIARY CONTAINS THE TRAVELS OF:

_____

9 8 7 6 5 4 3 2 1
Digit on the right indicates the number of this printing

ISBN 0-7624-1462-6

Interior and cover designed by Dustin Summers
Edited by Joelle Herr
Typography: DIN, Bodoni, Bickham

This journal may be ordered by mail from the publisher.
Please include $2.50 for postage and handling.
But try your bookstore first!

Running Press Book Publishers
125 South Twenty-second Street
Philadelphia, Pennsylvania 19103-4399

Visit us on the web!
www.runningpress.com

Traveler's Diary

A PLANNER, JOURNAL, *and* SCRAPBOOK

RUNNING PRESS

PHILADELPHIA · LONDON

PROPOSED

DATE

WHERE I'LL BE

WHAT I WANT TO SEE

HOW I'LL GET THERE

WHERE I'LL STAY

NOTES

ACTUAL

DATE

WHERE I WAS

WHAT I SAW

WHERE I STAYED

NOTES

PROPOSED

DATE

WHERE I'LL BE

WHAT I WANT TO SEE

HOW I'LL GET THERE

WHERE I'LL STAY

NOTES

ACTUAL

DATE

WHERE I WAS

WHAT I SAW

WHERE I STAYED

NOTES

PROPOSED

DATE

WHERE I'LL BE

WHAT I WANT TO SEE

HOW I'LL GET THERE

WHERE I'LL STAY

NOTES

ACTUAL

DATE

WHERE I WAS

WHAT I SAW

WHERE I STAYED

NOTES

PROPOSED

DATE

WHERE I'LL BE

WHAT I WANT TO SEE

HOW I'LL GET THERE

WHERE I'LL STAY

NOTES

ACTUAL

DATE

WHERE I WAS

WHAT I SAW

WHERE I STAYED

NOTES

PROPOSED

DATE..

WHERE I'LL BE...

WHAT I WANT TO SEE...

....

....

....

....

....

....

....

HOW I'LL GET THERE...

....

....

WHERE I'LL STAY..

NOTES...

....

....

....

....

....

ACTUAL

DATE..

WHERE I WAS...

WHAT I SAW..

....

....

....

....

....

....

....

....

....

....

WHERE I STAYED...

NOTES...

....

....

....

....

PROPOSED

DATE_____

WHERE I'LL BE_____

WHAT I WANT TO SEE_____

_____

_____

_____

_____

_____

_____

HOW I'LL GET THERE_____

_____

_____

WHERE I'LL STAY_____

NOTES_____

_____

_____

_____

_____

ACTUAL

DATE_____

WHERE I WAS_____

WHAT I SAW_____

_____

_____

_____

_____

_____

_____

_____

_____

_____

WHERE I STAYED_____

NOTES_____

_____

_____

_____

_____

PROPOSED

DATE

WHERE I'LL BE

WHAT I WANT TO SEE

HOW I'LL GET THERE

WHERE I'LL STAY

NOTES

ACTUAL

DATE

WHERE I WAS

WHAT I SAW

WHERE I STAYED

NOTES

PROPOSED

DATE

WHERE I'LL BE

WHAT I WANT TO SEE

HOW I'LL GET THERE

WHERE I'LL STAY

NOTES

ACTUAL

DATE

WHERE I WAS

WHAT I SAW

WHERE I STAYED

NOTES

PROPOSED

DATE

WHERE I'LL BE

WHAT I WANT TO SEE

HOW I'LL GET THERE

WHERE I'LL STAY

NOTES

ACTUAL

DATE

WHERE I WAS

WHAT I SAW

WHERE I STAYED

NOTES

PROPOSED

DATE

WHERE I'LL BE

WHAT I WANT TO SEE

HOW I'LL GET THERE

WHERE I'LL STAY

NOTES

ACTUAL

DATE

WHERE I WAS

WHAT I SAW

WHERE I STAYED

NOTES

PROPOSED

DATE...

WHERE I'LL BE..

WHAT I WANT TO SEE..

....

....

....

....

....

....

....

HOW I'LL GET THERE..

....

....

WHERE I'LL STAY...

NOTES...

....

....

....

....

ACTUAL

DATE...

WHERE I WAS..

WHAT I SAW...

....

....

....

....

....

....

....

....

....

WHERE I STAYED...

NOTES...

....

....

....

....

PROPOSED

DATE

WHERE I'LL BE

WHAT I WANT TO SEE

HOW I'LL GET THERE

WHERE I'LL STAY

NOTES

ACTUAL

DATE

WHERE I WAS

WHAT I SAW

WHERE I STAYED

NOTES

PROPOSED

DATE

WHERE I'LL BE

WHAT I WANT TO SEE

HOW I'LL GET THERE

WHERE I'LL STAY

NOTES

ACTUAL

DATE

WHERE I WAS

WHAT I SAW

WHERE I STAYED

NOTES

PROPOSED

DATE

WHERE I'LL BE

WHAT I WANT TO SEE

HOW I'LL GET THERE

WHERE I'LL STAY

NOTES

ACTUAL

DATE

WHERE I WAS

WHAT I SAW

WHERE I STAYED

NOTES

PROPOSED

DATE..

WHERE I'LL BE..

WHAT I WANT TO SEE.................................

....

....

....

....

....

....

HOW I'LL GET THERE................................

....

....

WHERE I'LL STAY.....................................

NOTES..

....

....

....

....

ACTUAL

DATE..

WHERE I WAS..

WHAT I SAW..

....

....

....

....

....

....

....

....

WHERE I STAYED.....................................

NOTES..

....

....

....

PROPOSED

DATE

WHERE I'LL BE

WHAT I WANT TO SEE

HOW I'LL GET THERE

WHERE I'LL STAY

NOTES

ACTUAL

DATE

WHERE I WAS

WHAT I SAW

WHERE I STAYED

NOTES

PROPOSED

DATE...

WHERE I'LL BE...

WHAT I WANT TO SEE...................................

....

....

....

....

....

....

....

HOW I'LL GET THERE..................................

....

....

WHERE I'LL STAY.....................................

NOTES..

....

....

....

....

ACTUAL

DATE...

WHERE I WAS..

WHAT I SAW...

....

....

....

....

....

....

....

....

....

....

WHERE I STAYED.....................................

NOTES..

....

....

....

....

PROPOSED

DATE

WHERE I'LL BE

WHAT I WANT TO SEE

HOW I'LL GET THERE

WHERE I'LL STAY

NOTES

ACTUAL

DATE

WHERE I WAS

WHAT I SAW

WHERE I STAYED

NOTES

PROPOSED

DATE ....

WHERE I'LL BE ....

WHAT I WANT TO SEE ....

....

....

....

....

....

....

....

HOW I'LL GET THERE ....

....

....

WHERE I'LL STAY ....

NOTES ....

....

....

....

....

ACTUAL

DATE ....

WHERE I WAS ....

WHAT I SAW ....

....

....

....

....

....

....

....

....

....

....

WHERE I STAYED ....

NOTES ....

....

....

....

....

PROPOSED

DATE..

WHERE I'LL BE..

WHAT I WANT TO SEE....................................

....

....

....

....

....

....

HOW I'LL GET THERE......................................

....

....

WHERE I'LL STAY..

NOTES..

....

....

....

....

ACTUAL

DATE..

WHERE I WAS...

WHAT I SAW...

....

....

....

....

....

....

....

....

....

WHERE I STAYED..

NOTES..

....

....

....

....

PROPOSED

DATE

WHERE I'LL BE

WHAT I WANT TO SEE

HOW I'LL GET THERE

WHERE I'LL STAY

NOTES

ACTUAL

DATE

WHERE I WAS

WHAT I SAW

WHERE I STAYED

NOTES

PROPOSED

DATE

WHERE I'LL BE

WHAT I WANT TO SEE

HOW I'LL GET THERE

WHERE I'LL STAY

NOTES

ACTUAL

DATE

WHERE I WAS

WHAT I SAW

WHERE I STAYED

NOTES

PROPOSED

DATE ....

WHERE I'LL BE ....

WHAT I WANT TO SEE ....

....

....

....

....

....

....

....

HOW I'LL GET THERE ....

....

....

WHERE I'LL STAY ....

NOTES ....

....

....

....

....

....

ACTUAL

DATE ....

WHERE I WAS ....

WHAT I SAW ....

....

....

....

....

....

....

....

....

....

WHERE I STAYED ....

NOTES ....

....

....

....

....

PROPOSED

DATE

WHERE I'LL BE

WHAT I WANT TO SEE

HOW I'LL GET THERE

WHERE I'LL STAY

NOTES

ACTUAL

DATE

WHERE I WAS

WHAT I SAW

WHERE I STAYED

NOTES

PROPOSED

DATE

WHERE I'LL BE

WHAT I WANT TO SEE

HOW I'LL GET THERE

WHERE I'LL STAY

NOTES

ACTUAL

DATE

WHERE I WAS

WHAT I SAW

WHERE I STAYED

NOTES

PROPOSED

DATE

WHERE I'LL BE

WHAT I WANT TO SEE

HOW I'LL GET THERE

WHERE I'LL STAY

NOTES

ACTUAL

DATE

WHERE I WAS

WHAT I SAW

WHERE I STAYED

NOTES

PROPOSED

DATE

WHERE I'LL BE

WHAT I WANT TO SEE

HOW I'LL GET THERE

WHERE I'LL STAY

NOTES

ACTUAL

DATE

WHERE I WAS

WHAT I SAW

WHERE I STAYED

NOTES

PROPOSED

DATE

WHERE I'LL BE

WHAT I WANT TO SEE

HOW I'LL GET THERE

WHERE I'LL STAY

NOTES

ACTUAL

DATE

WHERE I WAS

WHAT I SAW

WHERE I STAYED

NOTES

PROPOSED

DATE

WHERE I'LL BE

WHAT I WANT TO SEE

HOW I'LL GET THERE

WHERE I'LL STAY

NOTES

ACTUAL

DATE

WHERE I WAS

WHAT I SAW

WHERE I STAYED

NOTES

PROPOSED

DATE..

WHERE I'LL BE..

WHAT I WANT TO SEE...

....

....

....

....

....

....

....

HOW I'LL GET THERE..

....

....

WHERE I'LL STAY...

NOTES..

....

....

....

....

ACTUAL

DATE..

WHERE I WAS..

WHAT I SAW..

....

....

....

....

....

....

....

....

....

....

WHERE I STAYED..

NOTES..

....

....

....

....

TRIP ONE

DESTINATION
AIRFARE =
OR GAS _____ x _____ DAYS =
RENTAL CAR _____ x _____ DAYS =
SUBWAY / BUSES / FERRIES / TAXIS =
LODGING _____ x _____ DAYS =
MEALS _____ x _____ DAYS =
MUSEUM / ATTRACTION FEES =
SOUVENIRS =
MISCELLANEOUS =

TOTAL =

CALCULATIONS

TRIP TWO

DESTINATION
AIRFARE =
OR GAS _____ x _____ DAYS =
RENTAL CAR _____ x _____ DAYS =
SUBWAY / BUSES / FERRIES / TAXIS =
LODGING _____ x _____ DAYS =
MEALS _____ x _____ DAYS =
MUSEUM / ATTRACTION FEES =
SOUVENIRS =
MISCELLANEOUS =

TOTAL =

CALCULATIONS

TRIP THREE

DESTINATION
AIRFARE=
OR GAS_____ x _____ DAYS=
RENTAL CAR_____ x _____ DAYS=
SUBWAY / BUSES / FERRIES / TAXIS=
LODGING_____ x _____ DAYS=
MEALS_____ x _____ DAYS=
MUSEUM / ATTRACTION FEES=
SOUVENIRS=
MISCELLANEOUS=

TOTAL=

CALCULATIONS

TRIP FOUR

DESTINATION
AIRFARE=
OR GAS_____ x _____ DAYS=
RENTAL CAR_____ x _____ DAYS=
SUBWAY / BUSES / FERRIES / TAXIS=
LODGING_____ x _____ DAYS=
MEALS_____ x _____ DAYS=
MUSEUM / ATTRACTION FEES=
SOUVENIRS=
MISCELLANEOUS=

TOTAL=

CALCULATIONS

The journey of a thousand miles begins with one step.
—Lao Tzu (570–490 B.C.) Chinese philosopher

I have wandered all my life, and I have traveled; the difference between the two is this—we wander for distraction, but we travel for fulfillment.
—Hilaire Belloc (1870–1953) British writer

I have found out that there ain't no surer way to find out whether you like people or hate them than to travel with them.
—Mark Twain (1835–1910) American writer

Tip: Traveling with someone? If you pack half of your garments in your partner's bag and vice versa, you'll both have something to wear in the event of a "lost" bag.

I love to travel, but hate to arrive.
—Albert Einstein (1879–1955) German physicist

Through travel I first became aware of the outside world; it was through travel that I found my own introspective way into becoming a part of it.
—Eudora Welty (1909–2001) American writer

I travel not to go anywhere, but to go. I travel for travel's sake. The great affair is to move.
—Robert Louis Stevenson (1850–1894) Scottish writer

Tip: Troubled by airsickness? Remember that a seat above the wing is always less turbulent.

Travel makes one modest, you see what a tiny place you occupy in the world.
—Gustave Flaubert (1821—1880) French writer

If we are always arriving and departing, it is also true that we are eternally anchored. One's destination is never a place but rather a new way of looking at things.
—Henry Miller (1891–1980) American writer

Methods of locomotion have improved greatly in recent years, but places to go remain about the same.
—Don Herald (1905–1960) American writer

Tip: When renting a car, opt for a common model that is frequently used by the locals and request that all rental stickers be removed.

A traveler without observation is a bird without wings.
—Moslih Eddin Saadi (1184–1291) Persian poet

All journeys have secret destinations of which the traveler is unaware.
—Martin Buber (1878–1965) Austrian philosopher, editor, and translator

Half the fun of travel is the esthetic of lostness.
—Ray Bradbury (b. 1920) American writer

Tip: Always carry the phone number and address of your lodgings written in the local language.

Though we travel the world over to find the beautiful, we must carry it with us, or we find it not.
—Ralph Waldo Emerson (1803—1882) American essayist, poet, and philosopher

I met a lot of people in Europe. I even encountered myself.
—James Baldwin (1924–1987) American writer

It is better to travel alone than with a bad companion.
—Senegalese proverb

Tip: Be sure to leave a detailed travel itinerary with a trusted friend or family member back home.

A wise traveler never despises his own country.
—Carlo Goldoni (1707–1793) Italian playwright

A good holiday is one spent among people whose notions of time are vaguer than yours.
—John Boynton Priestly (1894–1984) British writer

The good traveler has the gift of surprise.
—W. Somerset Maugham (1874–1965) British writer

Tip: A hotel concierge can inform you of locations you should visit and areas you should avoid.

One always begins to forgive a place as soon as it's left behind.
—Charles Dickens (1812—1870) British writer

The world is a book, and those who do not travel, read only a page.
—Saint Augustine (A.D. 354–430) Roman religious figure and philosopher

Tip: Only drink bottled and sealed water, and resist the urge to indulge in vendor fare.

Never journey without something to eat in your pocket. If only to throw to dogs when attacked by them.
—E.S. Bates (1879–1939) American writer

If you reject the food, ignore the customs, fear the religion and avoid the people, you might better stay at home.
—James A. Michener (1907–1997) American writer

A traveler to distant places should make no enemies.
—Nigerian Proverb

Tip: Keep your eyes open as to where the locals like to eat. You will usually find good quality food at a reasonable price.

The traveler sees what he sees, the tourist sees what he has come to see.
—Gilbert K. Chesterton (1874–1936) British journalist, poet, and theologian

To awaken alone in a strange town is one of the pleasantest sensations in the world.
—Freya Stark (1893–1993) British adventurer

Even disasters—there are always disasters when you travel—can be turned into adventures.
—Marilyn French (b. 1929) American writer

A journey is a person in itself; no two are alike.
—John Steinbeck (1902–1968) American writer

Tip: For extra nighttime security, slip a doorstop under the door of your hotel room.

Keep moving.
—Hunter S. Thompson (b. 1939) American writer

I never travel without my diary. One should always have something sensational to read in the train.
—Oscar Wilde (1854—1900) Irish writer

The first condition of understanding a foreign country is to smell it.
—Rudyard Kipling (1865—1936) British writer

Tip: Wrap a thick rubber band around your wallet. The friction will alert you if your pocket is being picked.

With reason one can travel the world over; without it it is hard to move an inch.
—Chinese proverb

Those who go overseas find a change of climate, not a change of soul.
—Horace (65–8 B.C.) Roman poet and satirist

A man must travel, and turmoil, or there is no existence.
—George Gordon Noel (Lord) Byron (1788–1824) British poet

Tip: Think realistically, be flexible, and make backup plans for inclement weather or traffic jams.

I love to sail forbidden seas, and land on barbarous coasts.
—Herman Melville (1819—1891) American writer

On a long journey even a straw weighs heavy.
—Spanish proverb

. . . once you have traveled, the voyage never ends, but is played out over and over again in the quietest chambers . . . the mind can never break off from the journey.
—Pat Conroy (b. 1945) American writer

Like all great travelers, I have seen more than I remember, and remember more than I have seen.
—Benjamin Disraeli (1804—1881) British prime minister

Take only memories. Leave nothing but footprints.
—Seattle [Seatlh] (1786–1866) Suquamish chief

WHEN	WHERE	WHAT	HOW MUCH	PAYED WITH

WHEN	WHERE	WHAT	HOW MUCH	PAYED WITH

WHEN	WHERE	WHAT	HOW MUCH	PAYED WITH

EXPENSES | *Traveler's Diary*

WHEN	WHERE	WHAT	HOW MUCH	PAYED WITH

NAME

ADDRESS

PHONE

EMAIL

NOTES

NAME

ADDRESS

PHONE

EMAIL

NOTES

NAME

ADDRESS

PHONE

EMAIL

NOTES

NAME

ADDRESS

PHONE

EMAIL

NOTES

NAME

ADDRESS

PHONE

EMAIL

NOTES

NAME

ADDRESS

PHONE

EMAIL

NOTES

NAME

ADDRESS

PHONE

EMAIL

NOTES

NAME

ADDRESS

PHONE

EMAIL

NOTES

NAME

ADDRESS

PHONE

EMAIL

NOTES

NAME

ADDRESS

PHONE

EMAIL

NOTES

NAME

ADDRESS

PHONE

EMAIL

NOTES

NAME

ADDRESS

PHONE

EMAIL

NOTES

NAME

ADDRESS

PHONE

EMAIL

NOTES

NAME

ADDRESS

PHONE

EMAIL

NOTES

NAME

ADDRESS

PHONE

EMAIL

NOTES

NAME

ADDRESS

PHONE

EMAIL

NOTES

NAME

ADDRESS

PHONE

EMAIL

NOTES

NAME

ADDRESS

PHONE

EMAIL

NOTES